HAUNTED! ALCATRAZ

Gareth Stevens
Publishing

BY RYAN NAGELHOUT

Please visit our website, www.garethstevens.com. For a free color catalog of all our high-quality books, call toll free 1-800-542-2595 or fax 1-877-542-2596.

Library of Congress Cataloging-in-Publication Data

Nagelhout, Ryan.

Haunted! Alcatraz / by Ryan Nagelhout.

   p. cm. – (History's most haunted)

Includes index.

ISBN 978-1-4339-9244-5(pbk.)

ISBN 978-1-4339-9245-2 (6-pack)

ISBN 978-1-4339-9243-8 (library binding)

1. Ghosts—California—Alcatraz Island—History—Juvenile literature. 2. Alcatraz Island (Calif.)—History—Juvenile literature. 3. Haunted places—Juvenile literature. I. Nagelhout, Ryan. II. Title.

HV9474.A53 N34 2014

133.1'29—dc23

First Edition

Published in 2014 by
Gareth Stevens Publishing
111 East 14th Street, Suite 349
New York, NY 10003

Designer: Nicholas Domiano
Editor: Kristen Rajczak

Photo credits: Cover, p. 1 Chee-Onn Leong/Shutterstock.com; p. 5 inigo cia/Shutterstock.com; p. 6 Vitalez/Shutterstock.com; p. 7 iStockphoto/Thinkstock; pp. 8, 27 photo courtesy of Wikimedia; p. 9 Stringer/AFP/Getty Images; p. 11 Chris Saulit/Flickr/Getty Images; p. 13 iStockphoto/Thinkstock; p. 15 CAN BALCIOGLU/Shutterstock.com; p. 16 (John W. Anglin, Clarence Anglin) courtesy of AP Images, (Frank Lee Morris) Pictorial Parade/Archive Photos/Getty Images; p. 17 Cavan Images/Stockbyte/Getty Images; pp. 18, 24 photo courtesy of AP Images; p. 19 Keystone-France/Gamma-Keystone/Getty Images; p. 21 Albo/Shutterstock.com; p. 23 American Stock Archive/Archive Photos/Getty Images; p. 25 PhotoQuest/Archive Photos/Getty Images; p. 29 C Flanigan/FilmMagic/Getty Images.

Printed in the United States of America

CPSIA compliance information: Batch #CS13GS: For further information contact Gareth Stevens, New York, New York at 1-800-542-2595.

CONTENTS

Words in the glossary appear in **bold** type the first time they are used in the text.

THE ROCK

Now silent in foggy San Francisco Bay off the California coast, the secrets of Alcatraz Island remain trapped on its rocky shores. Once a military base and later a **notorious** prison, today Alcatraz is nothing more than a **tourist** attraction.

When the sun goes down, however, the eerie past of the island springs back to life. Deadly escape attempts and missing inmates mark the island's brief but deadly life as a prison known as the "Rock."

The story of Alcatraz Island is full of restless spirits. There are many ghosts hiding in the shadows, waiting for someone to hear their screams.

FIRST LANDING

The first people to visit Alcatraz Island arrived 10,000 to 20,000 years ago. The Miwok and Ohlone Native American tribes settled in San Francisco Bay before the first Spanish sighting of the island in 1769. Alcatraz may have been used to banish people who broke tribal rules. Many believe the tribes thought it was **cursed**!

MAP OF
SAN FRANCISCO BAY

Washington

Montana

Oregon

Idaho

Nevada

Utah

California

Arizona

Angel
Island

Alcatraz

San Francisco

Pacific
Ocean

San Francisco
Bay

Mexico

On August 5, 1775, Spanish lieutenant Juan Manuel de Ayala sailed into San Francisco Bay. He and his crew spent weeks making a survey of the land, including a 22-acre (8.9 ha) mass of rock in the middle of the bay. Alcatraz was measured at 1,675 feet (510 m) long, 590 feet (180 m) wide, and 135 feet (41 m) high at average tide.

The United States took control of the land from Mexico in 1848. A lighthouse was built and began operating on the island in 1854. It was the first active lighthouse on the West Coast. It could be seen from miles away!

FOR THE BIRDS

Alcatraz was first called Isla de los Alcatraces by the Spanish. It was named after the seabirds that were found there when the Spanish first arrived. The sound of lonely gulls and the **isolation** the water provided helped drive many **prisoners** insane during their stay at Alcatraz.

The lighthouse helped safely bring boats into San Francisco Bay.

7

MILITARY RULE

A fort called the Citadel was built on the island in the late 1850s. The dark, damp basement had rooms to hold military prisoners. They started coming to Alcatraz during the Civil War. The few dozen prisoners trapped on the island were put to work building other parts of the fort.

After the war, hundreds of prisoners were sent to Alcatraz. By 1900, a new prison was needed to house them all. Prisoners built most of the buildings on Alcatraz. While many still stand to this day, the first "lower" prison almost burned down after a few years.

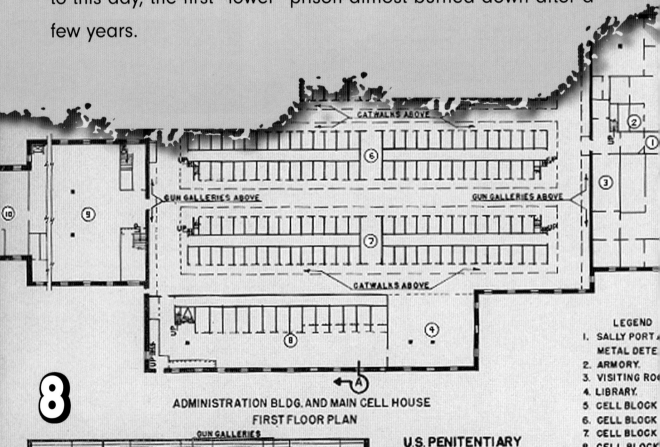

CATWALKS ABOVE

GUN GALLERIES ABOVE · GUN GALLERIES ABOVE

CATWALKS ABOVE

ADMINISTRATION BLDG. AND MAIN CELL HOUSE
FIRST FLOOR PLAN

GUN GALLERIES

U.S. PENITENTIARY
ALCATRAZ ISLAND, CALIFORNIA

LEGEND
1. SALLY PORT
   METAL DETE
2. ARMORY.
3. VISITING ROO
4. LIBRARY.
5. CELL BLOCK
6. CELL BLOCK
7. CELL BLOCK
8. CELL BLOCK
9. MESS HALL.

FIRST DEATHS

The first deaths on Alcatraz are wrapped in **mystery**. On July 9, 1857, three men were working when a huge rock slide fell on them. Two of the men, Daniel Pewter and Jacob Unger, were crushed to death. Just hours earlier, the area was said to be safe.

By the 1930s, many buildings had been built on Alcatraz Island.

During Alcatraz's years as a fort, a number of people died on the island. Between 1875 and 1910, 35 soldiers and prisoners died on the Rock. While 20 died from disease and nine deaths were accidental, five killed themselves and one was **murdered**.

Two soldiers' wives also died. One committed **suicide**. Another was murdered by her husband. Captain William D. Dietz shot his wife to death on January 28, 1891, then turned his shotgun on himself.

Another shocking event took place in 1909. Sergeant Roy Ford threw Private Thomas Mullaly out of a window, and he fell 37 feet (11 m) to his death. Ford then committed suicide by shooting himself.

NO REST ON ALCATRAZ

There was no cemetery on Alcatraz. Most of the island was rock, and there was no place to put bodies underground. Early workers even had trouble growing grass there! Soldiers were buried on nearby Angel Island, giving a few who died at Alcatraz a final resting place.

Angel Island was the final resting place for soldiers who died at Alcatraz.

11

ISLAND PRISON

In 1909, the Citadel on Alcatraz was torn down. Its basement was used as isolation cells in the new prison. Finished in 1912, it was used by the military until 1934. Then the island was taken over by the federal government for use as a maximum-security prison.

Alcatraz became home to the toughest and most dangerous prisoners in the United States. In 1934, the first prisoners were sent to the Rock. The worst of the worst prisoners called Alcatraz home. They were sent there by other prisons that couldn't handle these dangerous men.

ESCAPE!

As a military prison, Alcatraz often saw prisoners escape. In 1877 alone, nine prisoners made it off the island as part of "work groups" at nearby military bases. Other prisoners stole boats and left the island. Some were never caught! Others drowned in the bay.

The only way prisoners reached the island was by boat. One of the only ways to escape the island, then, was also by boat—or by swimming across the bay.

13

LIFE AT ALCATRAZ

Security was the only thing that mattered on the Rock. No one tried to make prisoners feel bad about their crimes. No one was made ready for a life outside of prison. There were no educational programs.

Prisoners were rarely given time in the yard. Very few visitors were allowed. The prisoners who came to Alcatraz even had a limit on how many letters they could mail.

The days were tightly scheduled, including meals, a few hours of labor, and "rest" time locked in the cells. Inmates were constantly under guard and, when in isolation, would have meals of only bread and water.

NO TALKING

Prison wardens had a rule of silence at Alcatraz. For many years, inmates weren't allowed to talk to one another, even while working, though that rule was later relaxed. There were no activities on the Rock. Many prisoners slowly went crazy, quietly watching the traffic of San Francisco across the bay.

14

Inmates could spend days at a time alone in a cell like this if they broke prison rules.

15

TRAPPED ON THE ROCK

The gloom of life on the Rock made even the most hardened criminal want to risk death trying to get out. Prisoners often worked together on escape plans. From 1934 until Alcatraz's closure in 1963, 36 inmates made 14 escape attempts.

Of those that tried to escape, 23 were caught, six were shot and killed, and at least two drowned. The remaining escapees are assumed dead, lost in the cold waters and rough waves of San Francisco Bay.

JOHN ANGLIN

FRANK MORRIS

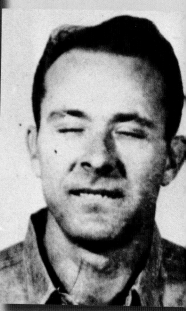

CLARENCE ANGLIN

MOVIE MAGIC

The movie *Escape from Alcatraz* is based on the June 11, 1962, escape of Frank Morris and brothers John and Clarence Anglin. In the movie, the prisoners used spoons to dig out of their cells, and built a raft out of homemade life preservers. No one ever found the three prisoners, but they are thought to be dead.

Icy waters and bad weather ended many escape attempts in death over the years.

THE BATTLE OF ALCATRAZ

The deadliest day at Alcatraz came in May 1946. Three prisoners—Marvin Hubbard, Bernard Coy, and Joseph Cretzer—started a riot and died trying to escape the prison. In 2 days, they let dozens of inmates out of cells and killed two officers, while hurting another 17.

No one got out of the prison, though. They couldn't find the right keys in time and remained trapped inside. Hubbard, Coy, and Cretzer were killed when explosives were dropped into the cellblock from the roof.

Two more prisoners were **executed** for taking part in the riot. Another was given a longer jail sentence.

SPIRITS REMAIN

People have reported strange things when walking in the hallway where the prisoners were killed. Night watchmen and tourists claim to have heard screaming, shouting, and other strange noises coming from the hallway where the riot ended. A reporter once spent the night at Alcatraz and claims to have felt the spirits who were still angry about their deaths!

This picture from May 1946 shows a guard pointing to where the prisoners tried to escape.

19

THE INMATES

Some of the most famous criminals of the 20th century did time at Alcatraz. While these dangerous men spent years in silence on the Rock, newspapers were filled with rumors of death and terror at Alcatraz. Today, some say ghosts remain. People have reported **paranormal** activity on the island.

Former prisoners have returned to Alcatraz and claim to have seen old friends who died years before. **Psychics** have had ghosts appear in cells and threaten them. Stories of strange noises and spooky figures all lead back to the men trapped behind bars on the cursed island.

THE TUNNELS

In the late 1800s, a number of tunnels were built under the fort on Alcatraz Island to keep soldiers safe in case of attack. Some cut through thick rock from building to building and lead to where guns were once stored. Stories say there are dozens of underground tunnels on Alcatraz. Who knows who—or what—is waiting to be found!

Could spirits be lurking in the prison's secret spaces?

21

THE BIRDMAN OF ALCATRAZ

Robert Stroud was sent to Alcatraz in 1942, long after he became famous for studying birds—and murdering a guard—at Leavenworth Prison in Kansas. Even though he wasn't allowed to keep pets while at Alcatraz, his nickname, the Birdman of Alcatraz, stuck. In fact, most of what people believe about his 17-year stay at Alcatraz isn't true.

Still, this dangerous killer's ghost has appeared on Alcatraz Island well after his death. People often see his ghost in the hospital area, where he stayed for 11 years while ill as an Alcatraz prisoner.

THE HOLE

One night, a prisoner in "the Hole"—an isolation cell—started screaming that he wasn't alone in his cell. The guards ignored him. When he finally stopped screaming, guards found him dead with marks around his neck. Doctors said there was no way the prisoner could have made the marks. What killed him?

Robert Stroud was much more dangerous than he appeared in the 1962 movie *The Birdman of Alcatraz*.

23

SCARFACE

Al "Scarface" Capone spent just over 4 years on the Rock. It was an eventful stay. The Chicago gangster had it tough at Alcatraz. He was moved there after using his money and power to get extra **privileges** at other prisons.

In 1936, a prisoner tried to kill Capone with a pair of scissors. Capone survived the attack but spent a few days in the prison hospital.

The attack took place in the shower room, where it was rumored Capone played banjo. To this day, guards and tourists claim to hear him practicing banjo in the shower room. They've even heard screams for help!

OLD CREEPY

Alvin Karpis was once known as the FBI's "Public Enemy No. 1" and spent 26 years at Alcatraz. Called "Old Creepy," he confirmed many rumors about the prison when he was finally released. Old Creepy said violence and crazy inmates were common on the Rock. Some called it the "Island of Hate."

Capone's stay at Alcatraz was brief, but people claim his ghost is on the island.

25

CLOSING TIME

In 1963, Alcatraz closed for good. In 29 years, more than 1,500 prisoners were locked on the rocky island. The cost of running Alcatraz was so high that the government decided it wasn't worth using the spooky prison anymore.

For years, the island sat alone, only visited by the ghosts of former residents and the salty mist of the ocean. Today, it's a national park. People can visit the island and look inside the old prison.

Many tourists have reported strange things on the island. Park rangers have heard closing doors and screams. Ghost hunters often come to Alcatraz looking for ghosts.

MURDER IN THE LAUNDRY BUILDING

The TV show *Places of Mystery* brought ghost hunters to Alcatraz who found paranormal activity in the laundry building. A park ranger later told them a prisoner was killed in the sewing room! Almost every building at Alcatraz has seen death. There are plenty of ghosts waiting to be found.

Are you brave enough to visit Alcatraz?

NIGHT TOUR

Millions of people visit Alcatraz every year. A quick ferry ride from Pier 33 in San Francisco brings you to the Rock. There you can walk in the footsteps of hundreds of prisoners and see the icy waters that never let anyone escape.

But the only way to get a look at the real Alcatraz is to visit at night. That's when the spirits come out to haunt their old home. You can even stay overnight with a group—if you dare.

Could you handle a night on the most haunted island in America?

ON THE SMALL SCREEN

In 2012, a TV show about Alcatraz explored the mysteries surrounding the creepy island. On *Alcatraz*, the prison was closed in 1963 because all the prisoners and guards went missing! They came back almost 40 years later, and a secret government agency had to track the missing people down.

Only a trip to Alcatraz at night can bring out all the ghosts of the past.

GLOSSARY

cursed: in a state of having evil or harm brought upon it

execute: to kill, often for doing wrong

isolation: the condition of being alone

murder: to take someone's life on purpose

mystery: something that can't be explained

notorious: generally known and talked about in an unfavorable way

paranormal: not able to be explained by science

prisoner: someone who has been captured or locked up

privilege: special treatment and benefits

psychic: a person who is believed to have supernatural abilities or knowledge

suicide: the act of killing oneself

tourist: a visitor who lives somewhere else

FOR MORE INFORMATION

BOOKS

Hawkins, John. *Hauntings*. New York, NY: PowerKids Press, 2012.

Watson, Stephanie. *The Escape from Alcatraz*. Minneapolis, MN: ABDO, 2012.

WEBSITES

Alcatraz Island — National Park Service

www.nps.gov/alca/index.htm

Plan your trip to Alcatraz, and learn more about the island's storied history on the park's official site.

A Brief History of Alcatraz

www.bop.gov/about/history/alcatraz.jsp

Find out about the Rock's jailhouse past on the official website of the Bureau of Prisons.

INDEX